You've Got Your PhD: Now What?

A Practical Guide to Landing Your First Tenure-Track Appointment

by Craig Winstead, Ph.D

Hawthorne Press

Copyright © 2012 Craig Winstead.

All Rights Reserved. Except as permitted under the U.S. Copyright Act of 1976, no part of this publication may be reproduced, distributed, or transmitted in any form or by any means, or stored in a database or retrieval system, without the prior written permission of the publisher.

Hawthorne Press
289 Jonesboro Rd
Suite 160
McDonough, GA 30253

ISBN-10: 0985431628

ISBN-13: 978-0-9854316-2-4

Table of Contents

Chapter 1 - The Curriculum Vitae (CV)

Chapter 2 - Job Search Strategies

Chapter 3 - Other Essential Documents

Chapter 4 - The Telephone Interview

Chapter 5 - The All-Important On-Campus Interview

Author's Note:

"You've Got Your PhD: Now What?" is based on the real-world experience of obtaining my PhD, searching for a full-time professor position while working as an adjunct, and landing my first tenure-track appointment at a university within nine months of earning my PhD. After reading numerous books, websites, blogs, and every other source that I could absorb regarding the academic job search, I developed specific skills and search strategies that I reveal in this book that any PhD working in the social sciences (and most other disciplines for that matter) can apply to his or her job search.

In fact, using the information contained in this book led to my receiving three invitations for on-campus interviews and two offers for positions at large universities. This book is mainly for those seeking to teach either in the traditional classroom format or in a hybrid model of classroom and online learning. With this in mind, readers of this book should keep the on-campus interview as their main goal. Below, I will share with you the tactics that will provide you the best chance for landing an on-campus interview and ultimately landing your first tenure-track appointment.

This book is not about shortcuts. I provide straightforward advice, real-world examples, and an easy-to-follow format without the typical fluff that accompanies many books on the academic job search. This book is written from the perspective of a person who has been in the same position as you the new PhD wondering what to do next. Unfortunately, many universities fall short in the area of career preparation. This is my attempt to fill-in the gaps and to uncover certain information that is not readily available to those who have not undergone the academic job search. Read this book, get that full-time, tenure-track job that you seek, and awaken the professor inside that you are waiting to reveal to the world! I wish you the best of luck in your search.

Dr. Craig Winstead

Chapter 1: The Curriculum Vitae (CV)

Every academic job search begins with one particular document. For those like me transferring from corporate America to academia, the Curriculum Vitae (CV) or vita (pronounced "vee-tah") is something quite perplexing. At first glance, it may look very similar to a business resume. You may even think to yourself, "I can just tweak one of my resumes to follow a similar format as a CV that I've found online." However, such an assumption may lead to your having little to no success in garnering the attention of academic search committees or job placement firms.

The CV is quite different from a resume and academic job seekers should see it as such. The more time you spend in the beginning fine-tuning your CV the better. For those of you who do not have much experience working in higher education, further reflection on your past business achievements may suggest many areas where you can nonetheless shine. As I highlight the most important areas to cover on the CV for the new PhD, think about how your personal experience may apply to the section. I will provide real-world examples taken from both my CV and the CVs of recent new-hires at large universities (HINT: many new professors willingly publish their CVs online and leave them open to the public).

Like resumes, there are numerous professional opinions of how to format a CV. This is of course dependent upon your particular background and experience. Therefore, I will not suggest any particular format in terms of how to display your information. However, I provide below the content sections that I believe are vital to the new or recent PhD graduate, especially those who have more business experience than academic. If this is not your particular situation, I congratulate you! You are unlike many and should be able to utilize your academic experience to your advantage.

Otherwise, I suggest applying the following sections at minimum to your CV: 1) Contact Information (this is a no-brainer, but I did not want to leave it out), 2) Education, 3) Faculty Appointments (if applicable), 4) Teaching Experience, 5) Corporate Training Experience (if applicable), 6) Publications, 7) Academic Preparation, 8) Work Experience, 9) Relevant Professional Training, and 10) Community Service. As a current member of hiring committees for new faculty, I can assure you that these sections cover most of what committee members look for in terms of your CV for hiring purposes.

Contact Information

Be certain to include your name (including your designation as a PhD), address, telephone number, and email. Job seekers sometimes choose to include a picture. You should not take this personal choice lightly. Some committee members feel that a picture helps to personalize the applicant's materials while others may judge the applicant in an unfavorable manner simply by the way that he or she looks. An additional consideration involves whether or not to include links to websites, blogs, or social-networking sites like Facebook or LinkedIn on your CV. I personally advise against listing such information, as there are always risks involved with what content may show at the very moment a potential employer looks at one of these websites. On a bad day, they may not see anything due to the site being down. In a worst-case scenario, they may see profane or offensive content posted by a friend or worse by you! For this reason, stay away from including such information.

Education

Present your education details in a clear and concise manner. You should include only degrees conferred by regionally accredited institutions. Be sure to include the type of degree, major, year conferred, and the name of the university. It should look something like this:

Ph.D.   Organization & Management, 2010, Capella University

M.S.   Leadership & Business Ethics, 2004, Duquesne University

B.A.   Theater Arts, 1991, Bowdoin College

If your dissertation topic is appropriate to a particular job application, you can include details like the alternative entry below:

Doctor of Philosophy (2010)

Major: Organization & Management, Capella University. GPA: 3.5

Dissertation Title: "Preparing to Move Recording Artists from Independent to Mainstream: A Collective Case Study of the Critical Success Factors from the Perspective of the Professional Artist Manager." Dissertation Mentor & Chair: Rubye Braye, Ph.D.

You can also provide a similar entry for your master's thesis if applicable. In any instance, be direct. This is not the place to boast about all of your academic achievements. Save that for your telephone or on-campus interviews.

Faculty Appointments

Faculty appointments include having worked as an adjunct instructor or assistant professor (or similar) at a regionally accredited college or university. Include the position, college/university, location, and dates. Assuming that your goal is to land a traditional classroom-based position, there is no need to include details regarding teaching online classes. If however you may also be teaching online classes, feel free to add this information to the entry. You will then want to include training for your appropriate Learning Management System (LMS) such as Blackboard or Sakai in the Relevant Professional Training section. Below are examples of faculty appointment entries:

Assistant Professor of Project Management, Saint Leo University, Langley Educational Center, Hampton, VA, Sep 2011 to Present (Tenure-Track)

Adjunct Instructor of Retail Management, American Public University, Charles Town, WV, Jan 2011 to Aug 2011

Teaching Experience

The teaching experience section includes a list of undergraduate or graduate classes that you've taught at regionally accredited institutions. Do not include any other kinds of classes taught. Be sure to list the name of the class and its corresponding course catalog number. You may also include the college or university name it you have taught at more than one institution. The entries in this section are straightforward. I suggest one of two styles:

MGT 430 – Business, Government, and Society, Saint Leo University

RTMG 201 – Retail Inventory Management, American Public University

Alternatively, you can list your classes in the following format:

Principles of Organization and Management (BUS330) - undergraduate
Goizueta Business School, Emory University

Organizational Behavior (MGT4100) - undergraduate
College of Management, Georgia Institute of Technology

Corporate Training Experience

PhD graduates in the social sciences often have experience working in large corporations. If your particular experience includes training employees, the skills gained from facilitating classes are highly transferable to teaching in the college classroom. Take advantage of this fact by highlighting those activities that relate most to the everyday duties of a new professor. Be specific about tasks and attempt to quantify them. See the example below of how to highlight your experience without going into unnecessary detail:

- Facilitated classes for seven years
- 3000 hours of in-class instruction
- Instructed students on 44 systems/products
- Led 2-day diversity seminars
- Lectured on quality management systems
- Certified internal auditors
- Taught New Employee Orientation classes
- Led classroom discussion groups
- Developed original course content
- Designed classes and wrote class syllabi
- Created testing and evaluation material
- Graded students in pass/fail courses
- Advised students on career and personal goals

Although your corporate training highlights will most likely look different, the basic premise is to suggest to the hiring committee that you already possess many of the skills necessary to navigate the college classroom. To be frank, some college and university representatives will overlook this information. However, it is worth placing it on your CV for the more enlightened crowd who consider such experience.

Publications

As a recent PhD graduate, I am certain that you have heard (seemingly a million times I bet) from your former professors and mentors that publishing is of utmost importance to new and experienced professors alike. Depending on the college or university where you eventually work, this may or may not be accurate. The ability to publish is critical to institutions of higher learning that place an emphasis on research. Often, these research-based institutions require full-time faculty to publish within a certain time in scholarly, peer-reviewed journals. Deans and department chairs of such institutions may terminate a new professor if they fail to not only meet the publishing requirement but also meet other obligations such as teaching load and committee participation.

However, many schools place an emphasis on teaching while publishing takes a backseat. The ability to publish may also apply more to tenure-track faculty as opposed to those professors who are not on the tenure track. In this case, your department chair may tie performance to student/faculty evaluations, committee work, and community service.

If you have not had an article published in a top journal, do not fret. You may still have some applicable publications. Consider books, magazine articles, conference presentations, graduate school paper presentations, articles in professional publications, working papers, or articles under review by refereed journals as sources for publications. It is a good idea to create sub-categories if you have multiple publications that you wish to list. You also want to cite your publications in either MLA or APA format. Below is a short example:

Books:

Winstead, C. (2011). Preparing to move recording artists from independent to mainstream: a collective case study of the critical success factors from the perspective of the professional artist manager. Saarbrücken, Germany: LAP Lambert Academic Publishing.

Magazines/Newsletters

Winstead, C. (2006). Five traits of a great leader. U.S. Postal Service Supervisor's Newsletter, 1(8), 2.

Presentations/Workshops

Winstead, C. (2004). Truth in information gathering. Paper presented to students, faculty, and alumni at the Duquesne University Capstone Poster Presentation.

Academic Preparation

This section is a straightforward categorization and display of your most important classes. You can customize this list to include those classes that are most relatable to a particular job opportunity. Please limit classes to those taken at the master's degree or doctoral levels. Try to categorize your academic preparation in a manner that would make sense for your particular discipline. For example, a business major may use categories such as human resources or management while a literature major may use humanities and modern American literature. Below is a sample listing of categories and classes for a business PhD:

Higher Education/Research:

- Statistical Research Techniques
- Survey of Applied Research Methods
- Advanced Qualitative Research

Business Leadership:

- Leading at the Top the Upper Echelon
- Leadership

Organization & Management:

- Managing and Organizing People
- Accounting & Financial Management
- Strategy
- Management Theory Creation
- Marketing Strategy & Practice
- Financial Resources
- Principles of Org Theory & Practice

Human Resources:

- Diversity
- Diversity & Culture in the Workplace
- Conflict Resolution
- Human Resources
- Valuing a Diverse Workforce

Ethics:

- Public Affairs Management
- Organizational Ethics
- Business Ethics
- Independent Study: Global Ethics

Work Experience

The work experience section is where many new academic job seekers often have the most trouble. The temptation here is to attempt to mention every successful business exploit and to list each skill or worse specific job tasks. There is a reason that work experience appears low in the list of headers on the CV. This is because most academic search committees are not interested in the fine details of your work experience, but are more concerned with big-picture ideas and experiences. It is much better to save those particular details for the various interviews in which you will participate.

In terms of citing you work experience, brief is better. The terms "less is more" comes to life in this section. Try to fill any gaps in your work experience with either self-employment or consulting jobs that relate to academia. I am not suggesting that you fake this information. However, do not forget to consider such experience when attempting to fill work gaps. See the brief sample below for formatting.

Founder/Owner, 2010 to Present

The Winstead Group (professional editing, dissertation coaching, and document preparation for graduate students), Atlanta, GA

Telecommunications Training Consultant, 2008-2010

United Telephone Technologies, Atlanta, GA

Web Documentation Specialist, 2007 to 2008

Verizon Partner Solutions – Access, Pittsburgh, PA

Corporate Training/Quality Specialist, 2000 to 2007

Verizon Partner Solutions – National Marketing Centers, Pittsburgh, PA

Relevant Professional Training

Beyond relevant teaching, corporate training, and academic preparation, academic job applicants should also list any classes that a hiring committee may find relevant to the job opportunity. Such training may include systems relevant to higher education (such as learning management systems) or any professional certificates applicable to the job. See the list below for an example:

- Axia College of University of Phoenix, Core & Specialized Faculty Training for online delivery using Blackboard, 2008
- SAI/Excel Partnership, Certified RABQSA Lead TL9000 Auditor, 2006
- KEMA Registrar, Certified ISO9000 External Auditor, 2006
- Eagle Group, Lead ISO9000 Internal Auditor, 2004
- Bob Pike Group, Train-The-Trainer Boot Camp, 2003
- George Washington University, Master Certificate Project Management, 2001 to 2002

Community Service

Hiring committees typically hold service to the community outside of the university in high regard. Therefore, list any significant volunteer activity or service to community organizations. Such service can vary widely from feeding the homeless to sitting on the board of a non-profit organization. Other examples include volunteering for the Special Olympics or professional conferences. The key is to make certain that the community service matches the values espoused by the particular college or university to which you are applying. Simply list your role, the organization, city, and dates of service.

Other sections to consider include Honors and Awards, University Service, and Professional Associations. Many new PhD graduates lack credentials in these areas at least as they relate to academia. If you are fortunate enough to have experience in any of these areas, feel free to include them on your CV. Choose a basic method to list each experience and keep it brief. Once you have an edited and clean CV, it is time to begin your search!

Chapter 2: Job Search Strategies

The internet is rife with job websites, directories, and search engines. Certain entities spend a great deal of money on advertising their services and optimizing their listings online. Some that come to mind immediately may include Monster, Simply Hired, CareerBuilder, and Indeed just to name a few. While these are reputable websites and many people find jobs by using them, they should not be the PhD job seeker's first choice for finding academic opportunities. This is true for several reasons.

First, many academic institutions choose not to use such services for full-time faculty and/or administrative positions. Often you will find with some rudimentary research that these institutions advertise part-time or temporary positions such as adjunct instructor openings on these sites while electing to advertise full-time positions on their own career websites, with job placement services, or on specialized sites for academic job fulfillment.

Second, several of the popular job search engines engage hundreds of thousands of job candidates who search their listings and create a tremendously competitive market in an already scarce field of academic job prospects. Third, this large applicant pool regularly produces an insurmountable list of potential job candidates for the hiring manager whose job it is to sift through them.

For these reasons, many search committees revert to traditional means of finding and hiring new faculty members. These tactics include hiring from within the college or university, asking for recommendations from within, advertising openings on their own career websites, or seeking the help of those who specialize in academic job placement. Therefore, my suggestion is to concentrate on four main areas when searching for academic job openings. These include academic job search websites, executive search firms, social networking websites, and professional affiliation websites.

Academic Job Websites

I recommend four particular academic job search websites to the PhD who seeks a full-time position. These include Higher Ed Jobs (www.higheredjobs.com), Inside Higher Ed (www.careers.insidehighered.com), The Chronicle of Higher Education (www.chronicle.com/jobs), and Academic Careers Online (www.academiccareers.com). I mention these websites based on the number/quality of job listings, the ability to drill-down to specific areas of interest by using an advanced search criteria, and my own success at applying for and landing job interviews based on listings appearing on these sites.

The websites mentioned above also allow users to register and save their CV to apply for jobs and make their CV searchable by employers who visit the site. Users can designate specific job searches and receive notification emails containing listings that match the search criteria. Email notifications serve as great time-savers to job candidates and may make them aware of opportunities that they may not have otherwise identified. Diversity candidates should sign-up for the diversity/affirmative action e-mail services offered by Higher Ed Jobs and Academic Careers Online. These email updates are a great way to stay abreast of institutions of higher learning that are actively seeking to diversify their faculty and staff through targeted job offerings.

A couple of other quality academic websites in my opinion are Scholarly Hires (www.scholarlyhires.com) and Academic Employment Network (www.academploy.com). Both offer valuable listings and allow advanced searches. I personally did not use these in my job search; however, I reviewed them for this book and like their design. It only takes one of these many websites to work for you. You will find that certain website designs will allow you to search for and obtain desired results more quickly than others. Take them for a test drive and figure-out which ones work best for your particular search!

Executive Search Firms

I know what you're thinking: "Executive search firms? I'm looking for my first position in academia. What can they do for me?" My answer to this question is simply "They can help you find the job that you seek!" In fact, the process for obtaining my job as a full-time, tenure-track professor started with an application to one such site. Contrary to what many applicants believe, several of the "executive" search firms while running search campaigns for universities looking to hire presidents, deans and the like also help to fill full-time professor openings.

Numerous executive search firms participate in academic job searches. Most of them serve a specific job market based on geographic locale. Therefore, the potential list is too large to include in this book. However, I will mention two firms that I believe are representative of high-quality executive search firms. These include RPA Inc. (http://www.rpainc.org) and Isaacson Miller (http://www.imsearch.com).

I am fond of RPA, Inc. first because I applied for my current job at this site. Moreover, they provide a simple and clean format for finding applicable listings and applying for the job, (they also provide the link to each college/university, which is useful). Simply click on "Current Searches" to view a list of job opportunities and then click on the job title links that seem to fit you best. RPA representatives typically collect all of your basic information such as your CV and college transcripts initially in the application process. They may supplement your original application with a questionnaire designed to weed-out job applicants.

This is actually a plus for you as a potential candidate because RPA will only submit to the universities they serve those applicants that have a great chance at getting offered an interview (albeit that it might be just a telephone interview at first). I found the staff at RPA very helpful as they allowed me to make a correction to my original materials prior to sending them on to the hiring committee at the university. This may have made all the difference in my application as I originally made the bonehead error of stating the wrong university name in my cover letter (a common mistake for job applicants, but not one I like to make).

Isaacson Miller similarly offers quality listings under their "Current Searches" tab. They typically boast a greater number of listings than RPA and seem to cover a wider geographic area. However, neither search firm will offer the number of listings available at academic job websites. Just keep in mind that these firms are working for specific clients who are actively seeking to make a hiring decision and who will take their recommendations more seriously than perhaps applications they receive uncritically from other web-based sources. In addition, the colleges and universities pay these firms for their assistance making it free for the jobseeker to use their services!

Social Networking Websites

Social networking websites are becoming increasingly important to the job seeker. This is especially true for those who seek a full-time, tenure-track appointment. I state this because the academic hiring process involves much more than the materials that you submit. It also involves having someone on the inside (preferably serving on the hiring committee) who believes in your ability and is willing to fight to get you noticed and interviewed for the position. One of the best ways to get to know someone on the inside is through social networking.

My minimal recommendation when it comes to social networking websites would be to make sure that you are participating on LinkedIn and on Facebook. I am certain that this is not the first time that you are reading such a recommendation, but I cannot emphasize the importance of social networking enough. It can truly make or break your career. You must begin to build your network long before you need it if possible. However, even if you are starting to network late in the game, it is better to start now than to not start at all!

LinkedIn is a business-networking website with thousands of members using the power of networking to advertise their skills to potential employers as well as to meet potential career advocates. It is easy to introduce yourself (or to be introduced through a friend or associate) to faculty members of universities including department chairs and deans that may be actively participating on hiring committees. This alone is worth building a profile and a network on LinkedIn. Besides this obvious advantage, fiends often send you pertinent job listings and LinkedIn offers a job search within the site that is excellent. There is no downside to building a network on LinkedIn.

Facebook is more of a casual networking website. This alone should not stop you from registering and setting-up a Facebook profile. Besides offering a personal profile where you share links, photos, events and other information with your family and friends, Facebook also offers pages that can serve to your advantage. Facebook Pages allow you to create a page that is viewable to the public.

When people "Like" your page, they automatically receive any updates or submissions to your page and serve as a community of followers of you and your interests. This is a huge advantage as you can tailor your updates to draw attention to your accomplishments and academic-related events. You can view a sample page by visiting my public professor page (www.facebook.com/drcraigwinstead). If you enjoy the content and want to participate in our conversation, please click the "Like" button at the top to follow my updates and make comments of your own.

Both Facebook and LinkedIn are free for most of their services. LinkedIn offers advanced searches and the ability to introduce oneself more freely to unknown parties with their paid membership. However, I do not pay anything on either site and use them to my advantage. There is no excuse for you not to do the same!

Professional Affiliation Websites

If you believe that there are numerous academic job, executive search, and social networking websites, you will be amazed at the number of professional organizations with which you can affiliate. Affiliating with such organizations can provide many benefits such as additional networking opportunities, job listings, conference attendance/presentation opportunities, and potential publishing outlets. These organizations are highly diverse and further the agenda of just about every academic discipline that you can fathom.

For example, if you are studying agriculture, you should think about joining the American Dairy Science Association (ADSA). You say that you are into drama. No problem. Consider joining the International Drama/Theatre and Education Association (IDEA). Business management? You too are covered by the Academy of Management (AOM). You get the idea. Whatever you are studying right now most likely has a professional organization with which you can affiliate to meet active members in the field. However, there are some potential drawbacks to these organizations.

First, they typically charge an annual fee (usually in the form of dues) to become a member. While I am not opposed to this fundamentally, not everyone can afford the fees as they can be quite expensive. This is especially true for an unemployed, newly minted PhD who is looking for a job just to first pay bills and to start repaying student loans.

Second, the conferences that they host cost money in addition to the cost for travel and lodging. This may be true even when the conference host invites you to present. Again, for the unemployed job seeker, these may not be a current option. Third, publishing in a peer-reviewed, professional journal may take a great deal of time (up to a year in some cases); therefore, the payoff is not immediate in terms of aiding the job search.

I am not citing these potential disadvantages to discourage you from joining a professional group. Weigh the pros and cons against your personal situation and decide if joining may be beneficial to you. If you need help researching professional organizations in your field, I recommend starting with the Academic 360 website.

Academic 360 is a wonderful aggregator of both academic job websites and professional organizations. To find potential organizations, simply click on your field of study under "Faculty Positions by Discipline." You will see a list of related professional organizations and links to their websites followed by current job listings. Could you ask for anything more convenient?

Chapter 3 - Other Essential Documents

I wrote about the CV in detail in Chapter 1; therefore, I will not restate the information here. However, it is important for you to understand that it is an essential document necessary for your job search. A standard business resume will not suffice. Other essential documents that search committee's will require during your job search include a cover letter, statement of teaching philosophy, unofficial transcripts, statement of research interests and philosophy, letters of recommendation, and an end of course evaluation or survey results.

Cover Letter

The cover letter should include keywords that you find in the job requisition. This is a basic principle applicable to all job searches. Employers use certain words to describe a position because these skills are required for the position and/or lacking currently in the department. There is an old adage that "People do not argue with their own data." This is exactly why you want to use the words and phrasing from the requisition.

It is also good idea to review the college or university's website and read their mission statement in particular. The mission statement is a gold mine of opportunity for understanding the culture of the particular college or university to which you are applying. Another great place to look for such information is in their value statement (if applicable). Values are at the heart of many universities and when you speak to them within your application, this makes you stand out as being a good fit for the institution. Be sure to mention your research interests if appropriate as well as your teaching interests. Also, try to humanize your cover letter by mixing-in a personal anecdote or perhaps something that you found of interest on the University website about one of the professors or even better about the Dean or another administrator.

Statement of Teaching Philosophy

Your statement of teaching philosophy should include words that are important to the college or university hiring committee as well. Again, you can find clues within the job requisition and on the website. A common mistake that applicants make is to submit a teaching philosophy that does not coincide with the philosophy of the institution. Be sure to understand what the institution looks for in a good teacher before tailoring your philosophy to the application.

Good topics to mention in a statement of teaching philosophy include how you view the students role, your approach to the classroom, how you address differing learning styles, how you utilize technology, the future of teaching, and how your background relates to your style of teaching. Your statement should be no more than one page in length. Anything beyond this may lose the reader and may make you look like you are self-important.

Unofficial Transcripts

Hiring committees often request unofficial transcripts for your Bachelor's, Master's, and your Doctorate degree. It is a good idea to have these on hand before you need them. If you do not, this may result in a delay in your application or cause you to miss a deadline. You also want to be sure that you find out how to request your official transcripts from each college or university that you attended. This is very important because each institution will most likely handle it differently. In my case, one institution required that I request my transcripts online via e-mail. Another one accepted requests only by fax and took up to three days to send them out. Both of these institutions had decent turnaround times and no costs associated with the request.

However, a third institution uses a service called Docufide that charges a $5 fee, requires a signed request (that I had to scan and email to them), and either will snail-mail the document to the institution or will send it to them through e-mail if the school is signed up for that service. The reason that is important to know how to request your official transcripts is that as the application process progresses and you get further into interviews, the hiring committee will request that you have your official transcripts mailed at some point. A long delay at this point in the process is a definite application killer.

The committee may also request that you submit a statement of research interests and philosophy. This differs from your statement of teaching philosophy as the emphasis should remain on your primary research method (i.e., qualitative, quantitative, or mixed-method), the specific topics that make up your research interests, how your research might add to student learning outcomes, and how you may include students in your research. Smaller colleges and universities are typically interested in including students as this provides the necessary practice in research if this is important to the institution. Your research statement should also embody the mission, vision, and goals of the college or university to which you apply.

Many hiring committees will also ask for letters of recommendation. Typically, they require at least three letters of recommendation preferably from former professors or other professionals and/or academics. I recommend getting recommendation letters from former professors both at the PhD level and at the Master's degree level. Make sure that you ask people who know your work well such as former committee members, mentors, or professors. Ask them to customize the letter to the position to which you are applying, date it, and sign the letter if possible (some institutions require signed letters). They can then scan and email you a copy.

Alternatively, they can send you a generic letter in Word with their signature included as a graphic. This will allow you to change the name of the department and the particular institution on your own instead of having to request that they send a letter each time you apply to a new job. Of course, you must have a very trusting relationship with the people supplying your recommendation letters.

End of Course Evaluation/Survey Results

The last of the essential documents include end-of-course evaluations or survey results. If you have not taught as an adjunct instructor or other part-time teacher at a college or university, you may not have course evaluations available. Unfortunately, hiring committees typically are not interested in reviewing evaluations from corporate or other professional classes. They should be from college classes taught at regionally accredited institutions.

If you have taught classes and gave out a survey at the end of class and/or collected data, include at least three recent evaluations. It is best to include just the summary pages with scores and student comments. If you must include multiple pages with scores on each page, then do so knowing that committee members may not review all of your information. This may seem obvious but be sure not to include evaluations offering negative student commentary (even if not directed at you) or comments that do not speak highly of your teaching ability.

As you may imagine, each hiring committee will request different documents depending on their particular needs. However, preparing these documents ahead of time will save you from having to create them on the fly (leaving more room for mistakes). This will also allow you to customize your documents to a particular application as opposed to creating each document from zilch.

Chapter 4 - The Telephone Interview

If you are fortunate enough to have the school invite you to a telephone interview, be sure to consider the following. The first action that you should take after answering the call is to ask the scheduler for a telephone number that you can reach them on in case you are accidently disconnected. This is of course after exchanging pleasantries. In addition, you want to be sure that you have your personal calendar/agenda ready as well as a pen and a piece of paper or your laptop handy to take notes.

The scheduler will most likely be pressed for time and will not take a great deal of time to fit you into one of the designated interview slots. Be sure to write down pertinent information such as the date and time of the interview, who you will be speaking with primarily, whether or not other faculty will join the call, and approximate length of the interview. Interview times vary from 15 minutes to 1 hour. It is common for interviewers to allow other faculty members to be present in the room while conducting the telephone interview. I personally had one interview where there were five faculty members in a conference room asking me questions at will. They may also have other faculty members ask questions towards the end of the call; be prepared for this.

On the day of the call, be sure to review notes that you have written regarding the college or university's history, mission, vision, goals, teaching philosophy, or values. It will be important for your answers to match the culture of the institution. You also want to be prepared with a few questions of your own that you will attempt to work into the conversation during the interview or that you save for the end of the interview if the interviewer allows time for questions. They will typically not allow more than five minutes for questions as they may be fast-approaching the next interview slot.

If for some reason you need more time before the interview begins (such as you may have to use the rest room or put a barking dog outside), simply ask if you can call them back in five minutes to address any distractions. Most interviewers will understand that you are probably at home and that distractions sometimes arise in this kind of situation.

Some interviewers will start with something like, "I'm going to ask you a series of questions and will leave time at the end to ask questions of you own." They may also break the interview up in parts such as a review of you resume followed by questions about the position with general questions left for the end. Expect the interviewer not react to your answers. Good interviewers will leave a small silent pause between your answer and the next question. Do not take the silence as an indication that you are not doing well. They are supposed to remain neutral and not react. Also, if you list any independent businesses that you own on your resume, be prepared to answer questions about that business! They will usually ask about your entrepreneurial endeavors at some point in the interview.

Before you get started, acknowledge the instructions for the interview and ask the interviewer how he or she prefers to be addressed (i.e., by Dr. or by first name). As the interviewer asks you the first question, remember to relax and listen intently to the question and try not to concentrate on your answer before the interviewer finishes asking the question. Researchers term this as active listening and it is always a good idea to practice during an interview.

Questions that the interviewer may ask you:

- What are your salary expectations?
- What are your weaknesses when it comes to teaching?
- What are your strengths as an instructor?
- What was your toughest teaching challenge and how did you overcome it?
- What made you want to teach at (XYZ) college/university?
- How would you teach (class name) in your first term/semester?
- Where do you see yourself at (college or university) in five years?
- What practical background do you have in (subject)?
- Has any of your work been published?
- Why should we hire you?
- What kind of classes have you taught in the past?
- Are you willing to teach evening courses?
- What are your plans for future publishing?
- Do you plan to keep your adjunct position at (institution) if hired by us?
- What do you believe is the best way to evaluate students?
- What is your teaching philosophy?
- What is your teaching style?
- What is your preferred research approach?
- How do you remain current in your field?
- Have you worked with (fill-in-the-blank) students in the past? (Online, military, adult, undergraduate, graduate etc.)
- Have you ever served as a mentor?
- How would you describe your ideal faculty position?
- Have you taught online or hybrid classes?

- Do you believe that you would make a good fit for this school? Why?
- What would your colleagues say is your greatest strength/asset?
- If offered the position, how soon will you be available?
- Is there anything else that we should know about you?
- Do you have any questions for me/us? (Of course you do!)

Some questions that you may want to ask the interviewer:

- What courses would I most likely teach at the start?
- What is the teaching load for new professors (i.e. 10 classes per year)?
- Will I be involved in advising students? If so, how many hours per week?
- What are typical class times (morning, afternoon, evening, weekends)?
- How long are most classes in terms of weeks (8, 10, 16)?
- How many full-time professors work in the department?
- In what kind of college or community service might I expect to participate?
- Will I be assigned a faculty mentor?
- Is there a faculty training commitment at the start?
- Is this a 9-month or 12-month contract (if not stated in job announcement)?
- Can you provide me a brief summary of the benefits offered by (XYZ College or University)?
- How soon are you looking to make a decision? To start?
- Can you provide me a quick "day in the life" scenario of a new professor at (XYZ)?

- Are there both tenure-track and non-tenure-track options for new professors?
- How long does it typically take to reach tenure? To be promoted to the next rank?

Take the time to answer each one of these questions for yourself prior to taking telephone interviews. Some general rules of thumb to follow during your telephone interviews include not talking too much about your personal life, never bad-mouthing previous employers especially if they were colleges or universities, keeping your voice up-beat/jovial, and getting across that you are a great person to work with and that you fit well within the institutional culture. You also want to be sure to answer all questions from the standpoint of how your answers relate to filling the particular role in question. The interview advice in this section is also highly applicable to those instances where employers invite you to interview at an academic conference.

If the interviewer asks something like "Have you sent over your original transcripts yet? You are in a great place. That means that you did well on your interview and that the committee will take a closer look at your materials. They may also go into more detail about the next steps or talk about why their institution is a great place to work. These are all positive comments. Be sure to have a few questions relevant to the position for which you are applying and about the school or department in general. You can ask for a basic overview of benefits, but do not expect the interviewer to go into detail. Even if they go into some detail, the Dean of the school typically handles negotiable benefits such as moving expenses or professional development funds.

I strongly suggest not asking about salary at this time unless the interviewer broaches the subject. You do not want it to seem like money is your primary motivator. The interviewer wants to believe that you want to teach at their school first and then talk about money later if offered the position. Besides, the faculty member conducting the interview often is not the person with whom you will negotiate salary. Some schools will be straightforward with a fixed salary range. This is more likely because they are aware that the amount that they are offering is below market level and want to know if you will continue with the process accepting that you may be able to make more money elsewhere. If the range is too low for your standards, do not waste your time or theirs by continuing with the process. Simply thank them for their interest and decline to move further through the process.

Chapter 5 - The All-Important On-Campus Interview

As stated in the Author's Note at the beginning of the book, your top goal as a seeker of a full-time, tenure-track position is to receive an invitation for an on-campus interview. Once you make it to this stage, you are more than likely one of a handful of final applicants under consideration by the hiring committee for the position. Enjoy this news for a moment and then get back to work preparing for the on-campus interview! This is not the time to rest on your laurels. While you are getting closer to a job offer, there remains much work to do before hearing those magic words "We'd like to make you an offer."

Upon receiving either a telephone call or email (more likely) requesting that you travel to the campus for an interview, pay close attention to the details. The coordinator should send you an interview schedule. If not, request this document immediately. The interview schedule (otherwise known as the interview itinerary) will serve as an agenda for you and each faulty member, administrator, or group of students that you meet with over the course of the 1-2 days that you are there. That is correct; you could spend as many as 2 days on-campus during the interview process depending on the institution and on the depth of the interview. This is a potentially grueling process so it is important to be prepared.

Many institutions work from a reimbursement system meaning that you pay for all of your travel expenses up-front while they reimburse you on the backend. Therefore, you should be prepared to have either cash set aside or credit available on a credit card to cover all of your expenses (including travel, lodging, and meals) for the on-campus interview. Depending on the location and number of interviews, the costs can run up into the thousands of dollars. As a modest estimate, expect to spend upwards of at least $500 for getting to and from the on-campus interview unless the campus happens to be within reasonable driving distance from your home.

You frequently will not spend as much on meals because faculty and/or administrators will invite you out to lunch or dinner and pay for those meals.

By the way, faculty members will tell you that it is "political suicide" to decline such invitations especially if they come from the Dean or other important faculty or administrators. While the situation may not be this critical, make every effort to attend any social gatherings to which you are invited. Remember, every person that you meet (from the maintenance person in the hallway to students) may provide feedback about you to the hiring committee. Do not make the mistake of making an off-color or downright stupid comment or joke to someone who you think does not matter in terms of the hiring process. You may be unpleasantly surprised.

The interview schedule will include contact information for the interview coordinator which many times is the chair of the particular department to which you are applying. It will also include an address where you are to meet your coordinator as well as directions from your home or place of business. It may also contain a list of preferred hotels, rental car companies, and airlines for which the University has an established discount. Try to make reservations using the discount as this shows that you are a responsible steward of funds (something that universities are keen on). Outside of this basic logistical information, the interview schedule will also include an hourly itinerary of meetings throughout the day.

Many times, you will meet directly with your contact/interview coordinator during your first meeting of the morning for about an hour. This is typically an informal meeting to put a face with the name, get to know a little more about you, and to help you relax before starting your individual interview sessions with faculty members. You will then begin to meet with various faculty members for half hour to one-hour sessions the rest of the morning. In addition, be prepared to interview with a high-ranking administrator such as the Vice President of Academic Affairs or the Dean of the school. He or she may want to gage your personality as a professor and may want to help sell you on the school if there is a question as to your intentions to accept the job if offered one. You will most likely end the day with a final session with your coordinator/department chair who may give you some early feedback on reactions from faculty or administrators.

Some faculty members who interview you will not necessarily be members of your particular field or department. They may be from a variety of departments depending on who is available at the time of your interview and whether or not they want certain faculty members to assess your skills and abilities. Some may not be aware of why the coordinator chose them to interview you. This works to your advantage as in those situations you can turn the session into a fact-finding mission about the school and about the life of a professor at that particular college or university.

There should be times allotted within the schedule for breaks and definitely for lunch. Use the breaks to prepare questions for your next interviewer or to rehearse your answers to their potential questions. It is a good idea to look at the names on your interview schedule prior to your visit and try to read some of their published articles before sitting down with them. It is also a worthy practice to discover one interesting piece of information about each interviewer. This should be something that is not necessarily academic but more of a personal nature that you can use to build a rapport with your interviewer. Often, you can find such information buried in the faculty bio of the interviewer on the school's website. You can also review their profiles on popular social sites such as LinkedIn or Facebook. It is astonishing how far knowing that a faculty member has a penchant for sports cars or high fashion will take a conversation. Keep a notebook with you to review names, positions, background information, and questions for the next interviewer while between interviews.

You most likely will not be able to use your lunch hour to prepare because faculty will ask you to attend lunch with them. They may also ask administrators or other personnel to join in on the lunch. Whatever you do, do not engage in gossip about faculty or other potentially negative conversation. In addition, you are not required to talk about your personal life if you are not comfortable sharing certain information. Simply steer the conversation into another direction by informing pushy faculty members that you would rather keep your mind on the interview process for the day and perhaps later share some of that information.

The part of the interview package that you may or may not see will be the rating criteria that each faculty member uses to score you following their interview. Traits that they will be looking for include your knowledge, values, teaching potential, and whether or not you will make for a good colleague. Try to remain positive and upbeat during all interviews. This becomes more difficult as the day progresses especially after lunch, as it is easy to get a bit sleepy after a (hopefully) good meal.

The Class Presentation

Either a class presentation or a job talk (or both) will appear on your schedule. If the interview coordinator is kind, it will appear in the morning as opposed to after lunch. This is probably the most important opportunity to show your potential as a new professor and you should view it as such. I have heard stories of applicants who did not do well in independent interviews but gave a great presentation and saved themselves from ultimate rejection. Just like the interview, the class presentation takes proper planning and research. Since I have not given a job talk specifically, I will defer to the many books, articles, and videos available by searching online to cover you on this topic. However, I suggest the following for giving a class presentation at an on-campus interview.

The interview coordinator/department chair will most likely ask you to facilitate a 30 to 45 minute presentation/class session for faculty, students, or a combination of both. In my case, I gave a presentation to only faculty at all of my on-campus interviews. The highest number of attendees for me was twelve. There are stories, however, of applicants presiding over an actual class of 25 undergraduate students, some to their surprise.

Therefore, be prepared for anything and always keep in mind how you will customize your presentation to fit a variety of audiences (you should at least consider how you would change your talk if you had to give it to experienced faculty as opposed to students) and situations. Remember, you may not necessarily teach in a perfect classroom environment. You may find that the only room available is a conference room and you are suddenly much more up close and personal with your audience than you may have envisioned.

Another caution is to consider carefully whether you wish to include technology such as an overhead projector, DVD or CD player, or applications that require an internet connection. Any such technology, while potentially enhancing your presentation, can also serve as possible pitfalls. For example, I chose to use PowerPoint at one institution and they could not get the overhead to work. Luckily, I printed backup handouts at the hotel that morning so I was able to go into my presentation without a hitch. Therefore, if you chose to use technology, make sure you have a backup plan.

Topic Selection and Outlining

The topic of your presentation will vary widely depending on the school's particular requirements. Some will ask you to prepare a presentation on a specific topic related to the open position and others will let you choose. If you are given the opportunity to choose your own topic, I suggest selecting one that either relates to your dissertation research or one with which you are otherwise intimately familiar. Be careful not to delve too deeply into your research and refrain from the overuse of technical jargon. Always keep in mind that your audience members may be students or may come from different disciplines than yours.

At a minimum, your presentation should include an introduction, overview of your talk, the body of the presentation, a class exercise that allows for audience participation, and a closing/review section. Your presentation should flow along with your PowerPoint slides (if you use them) in a seamless manner. Be sure to practice your talk out-loud while moving about the room and referring to the slides. If you do not have a chance to do this, simply visualize your presentation in the car or in the hotel room while you practice delivering your points.

It is important to outline your talk, as this will give you a chance to review for flow, logic, and clarity of your presentation. Provided below is my actual outline for a class presentation that I gave to faculty at Saint Leo University where I ultimately accepted my first full-time, tenure-track position. I chose to apply the basic tenets of critical success factor category research (my dissertation method) to generating factors that were critical for the success of a Saint Leo faculty member (quite fitting for the occasion).

30-Minute Lecture Outline – Dr. Craig Winstead - Saint Leo University

I. Intro

a. Introduction – Introduce myself, the topic, and why I'm interested (thank the school and say why I am excited about lecturing at Saint Leo (mention university values and how more schools should study and employ these, how u admire them), tell audience that there is **no need to take notes** because I will arrange to have the slides provided to them, (have a bottle of water avail) ("I'm delighted to be here...")

II. Overview

a. Background of Critical Success Factor Analysis
b. Definitions Critical Success Factors (CSFs)
c. Categories (CSFCs)
d. Practical Examples
e. Interactive Exercise

III. BACKGROUND

a. Foundation – **D. Ronald Daniel (1961) wrote an article on what he deemed the "Management information crisis"** based on failing defense contractor projects. Cited the lack of information collected to use in decision-making. **John Rockart (1979** coming from an Info Sys perspective) asked a simple but significant question in a Harvard Business Review article: **What are the real information needs of the CEO or any other top executives of a company?** In his review of management literature on the subject of information gathering and reporting, he found that **executives were not as clear on their information needs** as were functional or front-line managers. Thus, Rockart built upon the previous works of Daniel (1961) and Anthony et al. (1972) by developing a **CSF method aimed at identifying the information needs of CEOs through a series of interviews.**

(Theoretical connections with **Key Performance Indicators**, Key Success Indicators, Key Success Factors, (Drucker's MBO) his method CSF

b. **Industries in which it has been applied** - Researchers identified CSFs for use in management control systems (Anthony, Dearden, & Vancil, 1972), information systems planning and requirements analysis (Bergeron & Begin, 1989; Boynton & Zmud, 1984; Rockart, 1979), virtual project teams (Delisle, 2001), Department of Defense (DOD), program and risk management (Dobbins, 2001, 2002), Catholic elementary school management (Warriner, 2005), and more recently in strategic decision making of the Atlantic Coast Conference (ACC) intercollegiate athletic league leadership (Stroman,2007). Each of these studies along with a host of other important studies added to the development of both **theory and method in the area of CSF generation and analysis.** They also served as a testament to success factor generation and use across industries.

c. Benefits of the approach - **enhance strategic decision making by business managers. A top list of activities on which to track, measure, and report.**

IV. DEFINITIONS (CSFs & CSFCs)

a. **Critical Success Factor Category** (CSFC) - The identifiable planning components or elements that considerably increase the probability of a positive outcome for an organization, and on the contrary, when absent, significantly reduce the chance of accomplishment (They are the few key areas where things must go right for the business to flourish. Areas of activity that should receive constant and careful attention from management. Must be continually monitored, measured, and reported on (Rockart).

b. **Critical Success Factor** (CSF) - The specific activities or actions of CSFCs. These factors, unlike goals, are subject to change, time specific, and essential to the success of the business (inherent in a CSF is criticality and temporal nature, industry specific)

V. DATA COLLECTION/ANALYSIS

a. **Structured interview guide** – open-ended questions covering the 8 CSFCS

b. SAMPLE QUESTIONS:
1. What are the two or three most important activities that must go right?
2. Why did you choose those?
3. How would you measure those activities?
4. What are the constraints associated with each of these?

c. 4-steps – 1) list potential factors, 2) determine if used proper context, 3) count number of time mentioned (frequency), 4) sort/rank them in descending order

VI. CATEGORY SET 1

a. GLOBAL/INDUSTRY RELATED
b. EXTERNAL INFLUENCES

VII. CATEGORY SET 2

a. INTERNAL INFLUENCES
b. TEMPORAL FACTORS - determined by activities important to a particular organization for a certain period.

CLASS EXERCISE: ASK AUDIENCE TO GENERATE THE NEXT TWO SETS BASED ON BEING PROFESSORS

VIII. CATEGORY SET 3

a. RISK REDUCTION
b. PERFORMANCE

IX. CATEGORY SET 4

a. CULTURAL INFLUENCES
b. MARKET INFLUENCES

X. Review

QUESTIONS?

Take notice of the use of bold to emphasize certain phrases or key words. You can also use coloring or changes in font size to help you to keep your place within the outline. In either instance, I encourage you to create your own system to keep you on track. The worst thing that you can do is to try to "wing it" and go without an outline. Unless you were born to be smooth under pressure, take this suggestion to heart.

PowerPoint Presentation Tips

If you choose to give a PowerPoint presentation, follow these simple rules. Create a slide presentation using a customized background theme that either includes the school colors or perhaps uses the school logo. Try to refrain from essential to the success of the business (inherent in a CSF is criticality and temporal nature, industry specific)

V. DATA COLLECTION/ANALYSIS

a. **Structured interview guide** – open-ended questions covering the 8 CSFCS

b. SAMPLE QUESTIONS:
1. What are the two or three most important activities that must go right?
2. Why did you choose those?
3. How would you measure those activities?
4. What are the constraints associated with each of these?

c. 4-steps – 1) list potential factors, 2) determine if used proper context, 3) count number of time mentioned (frequency), 4) sort/rank them in descending order

VI. CATEGORY SET 1

a. GLOBAL/INDUSTRY RELATED
b. EXTERNAL INFLUENCES

VII. CATEGORY SET 2

a. INTERNAL INFLUENCES
b. TEMPORAL FACTORS - determined by activities important to a particular organization for a certain period.

CLASS EXERCISE: ASK AUDIENCE TO GENERATE THE NEXT TWO SETS BASED ON BEING PROFESSORS

VIII.   CATEGORY SET 3

a. RISK REDUCTION
b. PERFORMANCE

IX.   CATEGORY SET 4

a. CULTURAL INFLUENCES
b. MARKET INFLUENCES

X.   Review

QUESTIONS?

Take notice of the use of bold to emphasize certain phrases or key words. You can also use coloring or changes in font size to help you to keep your place within the outline. In either instance, I encourage you to create your own system to keep you on track. The worst thing that you can do is to try to "wing it" and go without an outline. Unless you were born to be smooth under pressure, take this suggestion to heart.

PowerPoint Presentation Tips

If you choose to give a PowerPoint presentation, follow these simple rules. Create a slide presentation using a customized background theme that either includes the school colors or perhaps uses the school logo. Try to refrain from using overly dark or overly light colors especially with regard to fonts. Use no more than 15 slides that you will plan to speak about for 2-3 minutes each. This will allow time for questions at the end, which you should encourage from your audience.

Include a reference page as the last slide and be certain to format it in the appropriate APA, MLA, or other citation format as according to the university's common practice for its students. Remember to bring a lecture outline and lecture notes to which you can refer if you lose your train of thought. There is nothing worse than stammering or creating awkward gaps in your presentation by using filler words such as "um" or "uh" while you attempt to decipher where you are going next in your discourse. If you run into a minor issue, try adding some minimal humor to calm your nerves and to make your audience feel more at ease. It always helps to think of a faculty audience as colleagues as opposed to a panel of judges.

Items that you may want to bring with you to your on-campus interview:

- A portable navigation device to get you to the campus on-time and to help you around unfamiliar surroundings in your off-time
- Printed maps with directions in case you have trouble with your navigation device
- Cash for expected and unexpected tolls
- Clothing for attending impromptu dinners or other social functions
- A pair of stylish yet comfortable shoes (you will be doing a lot of walking)
- A printed copy of your interview itinerary (make sure it includes the address where you are to meet your interview coordinator and a telephone number to contact him or her)
- A notebook as mentioned earlier to remember questions and to take notes
- Presentation materials (notes, slides, handouts on your laptop and in printed format)
- Backup slides on USB drive in case you have issues with your laptop
- Extra copies of your CV

- Faculty bios and any notes on the school mission, vision, recent news, etc.
- Answers to common questions on research, teaching, and why you are interested in working at the particular college or university
- A bathing suit if you enjoy relaxing in the hotel hot-tub prior to or following your interview day

Documents that you may be required to provide upon committee selection for an on-campus interview:

- DMV driver's record from your state
- State police background certification
- Values essay
- Official transcripts mailed (unofficial with you)
- Full HR application submitted online or filled at the school
- Teaching philosophy statement
- Copies of recent student evaluations with remarks
- Three letters of recommendation

Some Final Words of Advice

While there is no hard and fast rule as to how a particular institution will conduct their search for a job candidate, the guidance that I offer you here will absolutely point you in the right direction. Ultimately, it is up to you to put in the required research and preparation for landing your first tenure-track appointment. As I stated at the beginning of the book, searching for a job in academia is not about shortcuts. However, if you are willing to put in the work and actually take the steps to prepare, I believe that you will be successful in your search. I look forward to receiving an email from you stating, "I just got the job!" Who knows, maybe by then I will be able to help you to survive and thrive in your first year as a professor. I wish you the best.

About the Author:

Dr. Craig Winstead holds a PhD in Organization and Management from Capella University, a M.S. in Leadership and Business Ethics from Duquesne University, and a Bachelor's degree in Theater Arts from Bowdoin College. He is an Assistant Professor of Project Management at Saint Leo University. He worked for 12 years at a Fortune 500 company in both retail and wholesale; seven of those years as a training and quality management specialist performing content creation, editing, classroom facilitation, and ISO9000 auditing of both front-line employees and management executives. Craig also consults for telecommunications, music industry, and non-profit organizations.

Connect with Me Online:

Blog - www.drcraigwinstead.com

Twitter - www.twitter.com/drcraigwinstead

Facebook - www.facebook.com/drcraigwinstead

LinkedIn - www.linkedin.com/in/cnwinstead

Pinterest - www.pinterest.com/drcraigwinstead

www.ingramcontent.com/pod-product-compliance
Ingram Content Group UK Ltd.
Pitfield, Milton Keynes, MK11 3LW, UK
UKHW022213230426
12048UKWH00016BA/826